Diamonds Per Diem

Diamonds Per Diem

Affirmations and Devotions

First Lady Kimberly Todd

RBH PROFESSIONAL PUBLISHING

Southfield, Michigan

Publisher: RBH Professional Publishing, a Division of RBH Professional Development Institute

Southfield, Michigan

ISBN: 979-8-9893303-8-6

ISBN (eBook): 979-8-9893303-9-3

Contents

Amazing Grace

To amaze is to impress, startle or leave stunned, astonished. This is exactly what Gods' Grace does for me – it amazes me how freely He gives it; even though we don't deserve it. It bridges the gap between our guilt and His goodness. John 1:16 says it best..."from His fullness, we have received grace upon grace or grace in place of grace".

It's an endless supply that never runs out, even when we think we've exhausted it. The grace reservoir has even more in store for us! That's amazing!!

Note to self:

____

____

____

____

Life is Love

Another word for God is Love, it describes and defines Him. *I Corinthians 13, tells us that, "Love beareth all things, believeth all things, hopeth all things and endureth all things". Life=things!*

The absence of love (God) is fatal to a Christian; seeing that a 'christian' means to be 'Christ like". Christ-like means to resemble, look like, act like, to be similar, same way. Love brought us life, extended our life and saved our life.

Love is a fruit, a grace and a virtue; that can only come from God the source.

Note to self:

____

____

____

____

Memories Matter!

The mind has the ability to acquire, store, or retain and then retrieve or recollect information and experiences. Some of the information we choose to forget, while other information or experiences are pleasant and bring peace. Depending upon where we stored the experience/information; long term or short term memory bank – they can stay with us a lifetime or just momentarily.

...*"remember the former things of old; for I am God and there is no other; I am God, and there is none like me." Isaiah 46:9*

"Remember the Sabbath day, to keep it holy" Exodus 20:8

So remember the Sabbath, think on, meditate, acquire in-formation about God and experience who He really is through relationship with Him. On this day, all time space and energy to God the creator of you and the Sabbath. We will dwell in a space of gratitude; thankful for everything, taking nothing for granted.

Note to self:

____

____

____

Water in the Word

Water is necessary for the human body to survive; seeing the body is more than 60% water. Then to break down the makeup of 'man'; spirit, soul & body – we are 1/3 spirit.

We work so hard on the body part of us or the flesh, some of work on our souls (mind, will, emotions); keeping them in alignment – but few of us work on the spirit part of us. The spirit is fed by the Word of God, which leaves some spiritually anorexic, starved, and unhealthy.

Just as our bodies need water in order to survive, so our spirits need the Word of God to survive. We need Jesus Christ in our life!

"It is the spirit that quickeneth; the flesh profiteth nothing: the words that I speak unto you, they are spirit, and they are life." *John 6:63. I John 5:7 says: "For there are three that bear record in heaven, the Father, the Word/Son, and the Holy Ghost: and these three are one."*

Note to self:

____

____

____

____

I"m Taking a S.P.A. Day! Stop, Pause,

When we choose to take a moment to stop, pause, and appreciate what we have and have been taking for granted; it removes the competition spirit, comparing spirit, and allows Unity, togetherness, and gratitude to shine. It changes our focus from self, anxiety, fear, stress, worry to joy, love, and peace, which boosts our immunity and extends our life. We can then take bad news, hard conversations with a grain of salt, knowing God is making everything work for our good! God has blessed us with so much, even though we deserve so little.

A state of bliss comes from an attitude of gratitude. Let 'thank you' be the password before entering His presence with petitions.

Note to self:

____

____

____

____

Grace & Peace!

"**P**eace I leave with you, MY Peace I give unto you; not as the world giveth, I give unto you" John 14:27*

Grace & Peace was a customary greeting or salutation in the bible days; and still today in churches and temples. Once it becomes 'common', rehearsed, the words lose their weight, meaning, and significance, just as it did in biblical times. It was just a greeting repeated by everyone, so much so they said it even when greeting an enemy! Don't allow what you say with your mouth; not reflect what is in your heart.

Understand your words have weight, meaning, and power. Jesus Christ left a place of utmost peace (Heaven) and came to sorrowful earth – just so that we could experience the Peace He gives, not empty words the world gives!

Note to self:

____

____

____

____

12

Trust Fall

God never told us we had to be perfect, nor does He expect perfection from flesh. He knows we are going to fall and is always there to catch us and cushion the fall.

"Do not rejoice over me, my enemy; When I fall, I will arise; When I sit in darkness, the LORD will be a light to me". Micah 7:8-9

Falling, failing, and crawling are all prerequisites for success. The fear of falling can be counterbalanced with faith when we allow ourselves to fall at the feet of Jesus. That's when, in our weakness, we are made stronger and better.

Note to self:

____

____

____

____

Blowing Smoke

Most of what we experience on a daily basis is smoke, vapor; here for an instant, gone within seconds. Basically meaningless, not important, so don't sweat small matters. Ecclesiastes 11:8 "… And that most of what comes your way is smoke". MSG Blowing smoke is to brag on oneself, praising or expressing pride in your own possessions, qualities, or accomplishments, and feeding someone's ego with insincere compliments is referred to as 'blowing smoke up your skirt".

Be sure to rejoice in every day you have life, and don't waste time seeking approval, validation, or compliments from others, to make yourself feel worthy or of value. Trust God in all things, the maker, creator of all things – even smoke.

Note to self:

____

____

____

____

16

Know God Biblically

To 'Know' in the bible means to be in relationship with. *Daniel 11:32 "the people who know their God shall be strong and do exploits".*

To 'know' God is a powerful force against evil, and the influ-ential seductions the world offers. Having conversations daily (praying) with God; just as you would in any other relationship you're involved in – communication is key. Who wants to be involved with someone they never talk to? How are you ever to grow and evolve in the relationship if you never talk? Outside influences will most definitely pull you apart!

Note to self:

____

____

____

____

18

Seek, Look for, Search for Peace

I *Peter 3:11 Turn away from evil and do good. Search for peace and work to maintain it.* NLT "Seek peace and pursue it" NIV

Peace is absence of hostility, noise, war, to be balanced, in harmony; a state of tranquility. Free from what upsets or disturbs you. Stress-free, calm, secure, rest, stillness of heart.

The peace that comes from a relationship with God goes beyond the peace we get here on earth. *"Peace I leave with you, my peace I give to you, Jesus said, John 14:27*

The peace Jesus gives us has value that is unmatched; its worth can't be given a dollar value. The spirit, mind, and body all rest in God's incomparable, unequaled, peerless, and divine power. This peace can't be prescribed by a doctor, won in a lawsuit, passed down, or inherited.

The world can't give it or take it away; once you have determined in your heart to maintain and sustain it.

Note to self:

____

____

____

____

You are Seen and Vital!

Whether on the battlefield or guarding the equipment, every task, assignment, and person is a necessary part of the total success of any team, group, or organization. *Who will listen to what you say? The share of the man who stayed with the supplies is to be the same as that of him who went down to the battle. All will share alike." 1 Samuel 30:24*

To ensure you are part of a winning team, where success is imminent, make sure you are following the leading direction and instructions of God or His mouthpiece. *"In everything you do, put God first, and He will direct you and crown your efforts with success." Proverbs 3:6*

He promises to allow you to share in the reward, bounty, and blessings, no matter what role you played.

Note to self:

____

____

____

____

Obstructed View

What is in your line of sight? What is blocking or obscuring your view? When objects mask, or shroud your vision, it opens the door for uncertainty and doubt. Make sure you remove all that gets in the way of you seeing God clearly, hearing Him clearly and obeying quickly.

Sinful desires will blur our spiritual vision and close our eyes, ears and hearts to the truth of Gods' Word.

We don't yet see things clearly. We're squinting in a fog, peering through a mist. But it won't be long before the weather clears and the sun shines bright! We'll see it all then, see it all as clearly as *God sees us, knowing him directly just as he knows us! I Corinthians 13:12*

Note to self:

____

____

____

____

24

Perfect Peace (shalom shalom) in Hebrew

Perfect Peace is both a promise and experience. A promise from God himself as well as an experience for the believer whose trust is in God alone. The experience is a shield, barrier covering the heart & mind that cannot be penetrated by worries of life. This peace keeps us free from anxiety, because we lean on Gods' understanding and wisdom as opposed to our own. The confidence that comes from the safety, protection of knowing the Absolute, Faultless, Jehovah Shalom; keeps one in a state of non-disturbance, tranquility, calm, balance – Peace! Perfect Peace of mind gives a great ability to discern and separate lies from truth.

"Thou wilt keep him in perfect peace, whose mind is stayed on thee: because he trusteth in thee." Isaiah 26:3

Note to self:

____

____

____

____

26

Scarlet Red

The color scarlet is traditionally worn by cardinals in the Catholic church, to represent the blood of Christ. It is symbolic and associated with religion, devotion and sacrifice.

Rahab, in the book of Joshua 2, hid two spies sent by God (through Joshua); to look over the land in Jericho, that God promised to give them. Rahab a prostitute at the time recognized the God in them and had heard the testimonies of how He (God) had parted the Red Sea, and defeated kings that chose to be enemies of Israel.

She had reverent fear of their God of heaven and earth and chose to assist them. She hid them and when it was safe let them safely down to the ground through a window by a scarlet rope. She made them vow, take an oath that when they came back (not if); they would save her along with all her family. They promised that if the same scarlet rope was hung out the window as a sign of her loyalty, 'We offer our own lives as a guarantee for your safety'.

Joshua 2:14 Keep the scarlet red rope of hope on your person at all times as a sign that your God is the God of heaven and earth!

Note to self:

____

____

____

28

Fatal to Your Future

Offense: Easily upset or disheartened by perceived insult, causing resentment and bitterness of spirit. Often coupled with a negative attitude and unforgiveness. The greek definition (skandalon) is trap that holds bait or snare, stumbling block or obstacle. Offense is usually the cause of temptation and as stated in the greek definition, is what happens when we take the bait of offense we trigger the enemy's trap and become captive.

We perceive something that was never said, stumble over our own ego and get thrown off course – missing the whole topic, message, or meaning. Being easily offended stems from insecurity and inner demons we refuse to rid ourselves of through admittance and repentance. The paralysis of unforgiveness, bitterness and offense can be fatal to one's future by keeping them caught in a trap; unable to move forward.

Proverbs 19:11 A person's wisdom yields patience; it is to one's glory to overlook an offense.

Note to self:

____

____

____

30

Provision for Life

Provision from man feeds for a day; but provision by Jehovah Jireh provides for life. Whatever we lack or are in need of; Jesus sees and knows ahead of time. Whether it be food, money, employment, information, connections, healing, etc.

We can plan, save, store up for tomorrow; but Jesus Christ the Bread of life, provides daily. So pray your plans align with Gods' plan for your life. *"Don't worry about anything; instead, pray about everything. Tell God what you need, and thank him for all he has done." Philippians 4:6-7*

Note to self:

____

____

____

____

KIMBERLY TODD

Wear Joy!

Isaiah 61:3 *"to grant to those who mourn in Zion—to give them beauty for ashes, the oil of joy instead of mourning, and a garment of praise instead of a spirit of despair".*
Be intentional about what clothing you will wear each day. Take into consideration the weather, for example, on cold, dark, wet mornings (mourning); saturate yourself in the oil of joy. Then put on cheerful clothing of praise. Grief is a thief that takes and steals, leaving you at a loss spiritually after experiencing the loss of a loved one. Never regret your life due to the loss of another's life; don't live in regret and withdraw from living. Praise and worship the giver of life, Jehovah! He will sustain and maintain you through the brief mourning period, allowing you to reminisce and remember the good.
Note to self:

____

____

____

____

Pool of Pity

Swimming in pools of pity will keep you in the shallow end of life, never experiencing still waters of the deep. Allow God to show others your brilliance, passion, and wisdom for maneuvering through life. Pools of pity will have you overly concerned about the opinions of mere mortals as opposed to what God says and thinks about you. *"I praise you because I am fearfully (uniquely) and wonderfully made; your works are wonderful, I know that full well."* Psalm 139:14

You are unique, one of a kind, made in God's image – meaning you look like Him. God is perfect in all His ways!!

Stand on that and start living.

Note to self:

____

____

____

____

KIMBERLY TODD

Lend to the Lord

P*roverbs 19:17 "Whoever is kind to the poor lends to the Lord, and he will reward them for what they have done..* Can you imagine how well off you would have to be to have the ability to lend to the Lord? Whether lending peace, love, joy, strength, money, counsel, etc. The earth is his and everything in it, according to *Psalm 24:1: " The earth is the Lord's and everything in it, the world and those who dwell in it"*.

Remain in the heart space to be kind to others, especially those in need. The Lord will greatly allow the kindness to return to you in many forms.

Note to self:

____

____

____

____

38

Closed Doors

When God closes a door, as He did for Noah and his family in the Ark, don't try to re-open it. *Genesis 7:16 Then the LORD closed the door behind them.* It is closed, sealed shut for a time and purpose. If opened before it's time on the ark, the boat would have sank; Noah and family would also have drowned. Every living and breathing thing on the earth drowned, even non breathing things like mountains!

The closed door on the ark meant Rejection for those who had disobeyed God's instructions and Protection for those on the inside who had obeyed – Noah!

Leave closed doors closed, and walk through only the doors God opens for you.

Note to self:

____

____

____

____

KIMBERLY TODD

Others before Me

Choosing to love with an unadulterated, sterling, genuine heart is making 'self ' – less or last and others first, just as God did. He sent His only Son to die for us, putting us first, loving us first. It's humility and compassion in action! To concern yourself with others and their needs keeps one from becoming a self-absorbed narcissist. When your thoughts are always on you, what you want, desire, lust, hunger, thirst for, they can breed anxiety.

Loving others as much as we love ourselves is easier said than done, but it is possible. Anxiety doesn't stand a chance, when we put others before ourselves! *Philippians 2:3: "Do nothing out of selfish ambition or vain conceit. Rather, in humility value others above yourselves".*

Note to self:

____

____

____

____

42

Bask

Allow oneself to be exposed to warmth, light, bringing pleasure, peace, and enjoyment. Revel in and make the most of goodness, luxuriate, rejoice!

This is why Christ came, to bring us life, light, joy, happiness, peace, and to take away all of the opposite. *John 10:10 "The thief comes only in order to steal and kill and destroy. I came that they may have life, and have it in abundance [to the full, till it overflows]".*

So make the conscious choice to bask today, luxuriate in the presence of God.

Note to self:

____

____

____

____

Fall on Pillows

We all fall down, short, or out of God's' righteousness; but grace makes us right in his sight through Christ Jesus. His grace & mercy cushions our falls, whether self inflicted, life or pushed down by others. The cushion of grace and mercy makes it easier for us to get back up, start over, and do better.

Romans 3:23 says, "For all have sinned and fall short of the glory of God".

Note to self:

____

____

____

____

Fear is False

There was a song with the lyrics, "you've abandoned me and love don't live here anymore". That's what the enemy tries to get us to believe about God; who promises never to leave, abandon or forsake.

We are actually the ones' that abandon God until the first sight of trouble. We try to be ashamed to claim him around certain groups of people or say his name. Fear is false and only mimics what is real or true. Don't allow fear to have you lowering your standards and conforming to worldly ways and customs. Fear will steal your confidence, stability and security. Tell fear, "I've abandoned you, fear is not welcomed here anymore".

"Yea, though I walk through the valley of the shadow of death, I will fear no evil: for thou art with me; thy rod and thy staff they comfort me". Psalm 23:4
Note to self:

48

Say What I Say

To put God in remembrance of His Word is to repeat what He says in His Word. If we never read His Word, we won't know what it says. Out of the abundance of the heart the mouth speaks. So pray that you are filled to the brim with the Word of God, so that the words will flow out of you like a river of life.

"Put me in remembrance; let us plead together: declare thou, that thou mayest be justified". Isaiah 43:26

For God to say, "let us plead together", is an invitation to join forces with Him, declare, decree, repeat His Word, with all of heaven backing you, and watch it come to pass!

Note to self:

____

____

____

50

Ranking your Rivals

Be sure not to rank Jesus Christ as one of your perceived rivals, putting him on an opponent or competitor list. He should never have to compete with anyone or anything to get your attention and love, in response to the unconditional love He gives. Nothing and no one can compete, compare, or be in contest with Jesus.

Based on the comparative analysis found in the Word of God; He has no rivals, equals, competitors, contenders, or challengers. He is all-powerful (omnipotent), all-knowing (omniscient), Absolute, I AM WHO I AM, Elohim! Pharisees thought that laws could save them; position and status were paramount to them. 41-44 "I'm not interested in crowd approval. And do you know why? Because I know you and your crowds.

I know that love, especially God's love, is not on your working agenda. I came with the authority of my Father, and you either dismiss me or avoid me. If another came, acting self-important, you would welcome him with open arms. How do you expect to get anywhere with God when you spend all your time jockeying for position with each other, ranking your rivals and ignoring God? John 5:41-44 MSG

Note to self:

____

____

____

52

Remembered and Admired

J esus Christ the Son of God, should be remembered and admired. Not mere mortals, flesh, temporal beings, created beings. *In the book of Matthew 26:13 "You can be sure that wherever in the whole world the Message is preached, what she has just done is going to be remembered and admired.".*

Jesus Christ gave his life to save our lives, this act making the statement that "we are to die for"! This is love on an extreme level; such that will never be witnessed again by a human, mortal being.

The attention and admiration showered on people of position, power, or authority is idol worship and will be punished at its' set time. ...*"that at the name of Jesus every knee should bow, of those in heaven, and of those on earth, and of those under the earth, 11 and that every tongue should confess that Jesus Christ is Lord, to the glory of God the Father".* *Philippians 2:10-11*

Note to self:

____

____

____

____

54

Three Stand Cord

There is strength in numbers, especially three. *"Though one may be overpowered, two can defend themselves. A cord of three strands is not quickly broken". Ecclesiastes 4:12*
Advice to husband and wife: keep God woven into the center of your union. Keep opinions, input, and suggestions from all third parties at bay, no matter who is trying to insert themselves. A married covenant couple is two individuals, man and wife, and the only welcomed third party is God, the core and nucleus. Having God at the center is fundamental to bringing stability and longevity, positively charging and empowering the marriage bond.

Note to self:

____

____

____

____

56

Finish Strong

Resist the feeling to quit, faint, give up, give in to a feeling of tiredness, boredom, or discouragement. *Galatians 6:9 says, "And let us not grow weary of doing good, for in due season we will reap, if we do not give up"*. Never allow yourself to grow tired of doing what is right, good, and best for all involved – tell the flesh to hush! When running a race, we all have the tendency and temptation to quit, give up, stop; but then a thought of all the hard work, training, and discipline comes to mind. I can't stop and won't stop until I reach the end and claim my prize, reward. Let God be the wind that gives you wings, strength, endurance – stay the race, course so at least you can say, "I did not quit"!

Note to self:

____

____

____

____

58

Word Walls

Excessive words build a soundproof wall – nothing gets in; instruction, logic, understanding, explaining…

Excessive, unrestrained, unbridled, superfluous words show a lack of self-discipline, control; which is a fruit of the spirit. If you can't control your tongue, you more than likely show poor management or lack of discipline in other aspects of your life. More talk, less truth – so Proverbs 10:19 advises. Let's start with being quick to hear, listening intentionally for details; then thinking before speaking; responding – this shows wisdom & maturity!

Note to self:

____

____

____

____

60

WWJD - What would Jesus do?

"*They followed worthless idols and became worthless themselves*". *Jeremiah 2:5.* Whatever moves, leads or proceeds you is what you become. Anything that obstructs your view, is large in front of you on a consistent basis; is what you will model yourself after. Let Jesus obstruct your view to the point all you see is him, and desire to act like, love like, speak like him. It may not be the popular path; but it renders a great harvest.

Note to self:

____

____

____

____

62

Full Speed Ahead

Honesty, nobility lives confident and carefree; while sketchy, mendacious, deceitful person cannot move forward constantly having to look back, behind them. Their ways will be exposed. *Proverbs 10:9 'Whoever walks in integrity walks securely, but whoever takes crooked paths will be found out" NIV*

Note to self:

____

____

____

____

64

NSF- Non-sufficient Funds

Non-sufficient funds is a banking term indicating that the account lacks enough money to cover the transaction or payment, or has low activity.

We never want our prayers or petitions to God to return to us, due to a lack of time spent with God. Does he recognize your voice, know your name? To 'know' in the Bible means to be in a relationship with, intimately. One day the evil spirit answered them, *"Jesus I know, and Paul I know about, but who are you?" Acts 19:15*

You cannot have an intimate relationship with someone you don't spend time with, getting to know them. Don't allow an inactive prayer life to close your account in heaven, causing your prayers to bounce back unanswered.

Note to self:

____

____

____

____

66

Take a Seat

Take a seat at the feet of Jesus and find real rest among other blessings like water for a soul that's thirsty, energy from weariness and grace upon more grace. Taking a seat is a posture; essentially taking a knee in humility, surrendering all, listening and learning. The hustle and bustle of life, can have us too rushed to stop and see just how good God has been.

Isaiah 40:30 "They that wait upon the Lord will get new strength". Sit at his feet, regain your composure and new strength, energy, and insight to keep going with God.

Note to self:

____

____

____

____

68

Mountains become Flat

When God goes before us, paving paths, making what is crooked straight; life takes on a new trajectory. Life will be life, bringing with it tests, trials and challenges; however, God the creator, has the ability to remove obstacles, giants, oppositions – making those mountains flat. Mountains are huge in appearance, making them seem to be insurmountable or an unmovable barrier. *God promises in Isaiah 45:2 "I will go before you and level the mountains, I will break down gates of bronze and cut through bars of iron".*

When mountains are made flat you can then walk right over them with little to no effort. Gates are opened, and bars cut; welcoming your entrance or exit if they imprisoned or held you in bondage.

So start the day by sending Judah, Tehillah (Hebrew), praise before you; acknowledging Jehovah as King!

Note to self:

____

____

____

____

Sunshine & Rain = Friends!

Appreciate both the sun and rain in your life; both are necessary for growth. Independent of one another, will cause one to drown or dry up. We derive nutrients from sunlight and Jesus Christ {Son light}, along with heat, which warms to keep from freezing. Rain is the water necessary to quench, moisten and alleviate thirst. Both go hand in hand, fostering growth and development. Let us acknowledge the Lord; let us press on to acknowledge him. *As surely as the sun rises, he will appear: he will come to us like the winter rains, like the spring rains that water the earth. Hosea 6:3*

Note to self:

72

Laser Beams

Intense, narrow, focused light acting in coherence (same direction), that can cut through steel or perform surgery, is a laser beam. The beams cause instant damage to the eye in under 10 seconds if looked at directly! The radiance of God's Glory is what lights up heaven, leaving no need for lamps or sunlight. *Revelation 21:23"...by its' light nations will walk"*

Allow God's Glory to burn off everything that doesn't look like him, refine and purify, revealing the beauty of holiness in you.

Note to self:

____

____

____

____

KIMBERLY TODD

Sow Seeds not Weeds

Weeds take the space intended for something good. Sow seeds, pluck the weeds, and look forward to a harvest of goodness in abundance. Deeds done here on earth are seeds sown into eternity. Be kind and render good; treat others as you would like to be treated. You will reap a harvest here as well as eternity.

Galatians 6:7 "Do not be deceived: God is not mocked, for whatever one sows, that will he also reap."

Note to self:

____

____

____

____

Silence is Golden

Silence is a discipline, an art that has to be learned and practiced. *"When words are many, transgression is not lacking, but whoever restrains his lips is prudent".* Proverbs 10:19. *"There is a time for silence, and a time to speak"* Ecclesiastes 3:7

Note to self:

____

____

____

____

78

Trouble Looks for You

We don't just 'get' into trouble; it looks for and has to find us, when we make it a habit of causing trouble for others. *"The Lord will give trouble to those who trouble you". Proverbs 11:21.* When facing hardship or adversity; be encouraged to know that God remains faithful in his plan for you; his justice will prevail.

Note to self:

____

____

____

____

80

Wolf Dressed as Sheep

It takes a lot of effort for a wolf to dress up as a sheep. He has to put on layers of wool and after some time gets too hot, and starts to unveil his true identity and sharp teeth. The wolves eat the sheep in order to get their wool. Allow your discerning spirit to determine whether a person is really who they present themselves as. Opportunists, false prophets, fake people present themselves to be well-meaning and harmless; all the while actually deceitful and dangerous.

"Beware of false prophets, who come to you in sheep's clothing, but inwardly they are ravenous wolves. You will know them by their fruits." Matthew 7:15

Look for the fruit in a persons' life; love, joy, peace, patience, kindness, goodness, faithfulness, gentleness and self-control (tongue). If you don't see any fruit and only poison, toxins coming from them – run!

Note to self:

____

____

____

____

Light Leads

Light goes before and paves a path; whereas, darkness stops, paralyzes, and imputes fear. Darkness conceals, hides, danger that could be unseen objects, creatures, or people, that can bring harm or injury. Allow the light of God to dominate darkness, knowing that, *"Your word is a lamp to my feet and a light to my path" Psalm 119:105*

Note to self:

____

____

____

____

84

No Whining, I'm Winning!

When you shift your focus to winning; it leaves little to no time for whining. Jehovah Nissi is another name for God, meaning 'the Lord is my banner'. Exodus 17:15 It represents the presence of God as protector; bring victory and triumph due to his presence. Know that you are never alone, he is always with us as an ever-present help when needed.

The time it takes to complain or whine about circumstances is wasted when it can be spent praising God. He let us know the end of the story at the beginning, assuring us that we will always be victorious in battles, trials, and hardship. Just keep focusing on Jehovah Nissi!

Note to self:

____

____

____

____

86

Failure, Not an Option

In times of perceived failure, God's Word comes to remind us that 'failure is not an option'. This stance of determination lets us know we all fall, but it is not a permanent state. *Romans 3:23 says, "For all have sinned and fall short of the glory of God."*

Some of the greatest successors fall, lose, stumble, but it is all about the 'get up'. Follow this business plan: *"Commit your actions to the Lord, and your plans will succeed." Proverbs 16:3.*

Note to self:

____

____

____

____

Tried faith $=$ Patience

Patience blossoms into a beautiful bouquet when our faith is tried. It works and peels off so many heavy, burdensome layers; leaving us free to bloom. Burdens and worries are like carrying backpacks full of bricks. Lighten your load, pray about it, give it to Jesus; He has been asking to carry it anyway, knowing nothing is too heavy for him.

Have the faith that it is going to happen for your good, no matter how dense the fog of the future seems. You don't yet see it, but faith is hoping in the unseen.

Now faith, is the substance of things hoped for, evidenced by what is not seen. Hebrews 11:1

Note to self:

____

____

____

____

90

Reflection Inspection

Give serious thought or consideration; look at an image in the mirror, all with careful examination = reflect or inspect. As a representative of God, his ambassador, one must do a self-reflection inspection, making it personal. Being part of a royal priesthood as children of God means conducting and carrying ourselves as such. We have a great lineage and reputation to uphold. What are people saying about us when we are not around? Self-reflection fosters personal growth and a desire to align with God's will.

"Examine yourselves, whether you are in the faith; prove your own selves." 2 Corinthians 13:5 This verse encourages people to actively assess their own faith and actions, which is a key component of self-reflection.

Note to self:

____

____

____

____

KIMBERLY TODD

How Fit are You?

Concentrating on the physical state of being, i.e., eating healthy, exercising, eight hours of sleep, etc., only will invite imbalance into our lives. Just as we eat fruits, vegetables, and grains daily, we need to feed the spirit man with prayer, praise, and worship, and make sure the fruit of the spirit is noticed by others, daily. For physical training is of some value, but godliness has value for all things, holding promise for both the present life and the life to come. *I Timothy 4:8. When there is balance in our lives of the spirit and natural man; peace and harmony are second nature, which extends our life.*

Note to self:

____

____

____

____

94

God is Constant

God is the only constant in an ever-changing world. Wasting time trying to keep up with the trends, popular viewpoints, and opinions can make a person dizzy. People change like we change clothing – changing the mind, friends, commitments, even gods! Stop spinning, being tossed to and fro, and just focus. Focus on the constant foundation of Jesus Christ.

"Every good and perfect gift is from above, coming down from the Father of the heavenly lights, who does not change like shifting shadows." James 1:17

Note to self:

____

____

____

____

96

Fear Fights Faith

Fear is not of God and when left to foster and grow, breeds anxiety. Anxiety comes with enough issues of its' own, causing mental breakdowns, physical ailments, emotional and chemical imbalances and more. *Philippians 4:6-7 says, "Do not be anxious about anything, but in everything by prayer and petition, with thanksgiving, present your requests to God. And the peace of God, which transcends all understanding, will guard your hearts and your minds in Christ Jesus".*

Invite the light (Jesus Christ) the way, truth and light into your life. His light casts out all fear, doubt and unbelief. Choose your battles and don't let fear be one of them. That fight (battle) has already been won by Jesus Christ!

Note to self:

____

____

____

____

98

Complacency Zone

Humans have the tendency to default to a safe space, comfort zone, or controlled climate. *Joshua 1:9 says, "Have not I com-manded you? Be strong and of a good courage; be not afraid, neither be thou dismayed: for the Lord thy God is with thee whithersoever thou goest."*

When life brings you to a 'bungy jump' experience, where you feel fear in the beginning; but thrilled, empowered and free afterwards; open your heart and mind. Allow God to lead and be in control; out front, upholding you, in that career change, move to a new state or country, giving your testimony to a non-believer, etc. Step outside that complacency, comfort zone into your divine potential zone and make an impact for God!

Note to self:

____

____

____

____

RSVP

'R'SVP' is a French expression meaning to "please respond" or reserve your seat or confirm attendance from an invitation. God is constantly extending invites to us no matter our status in life. The least we can do is to respond, RSVP – it is rude when we don't.

RSVP, respond, reserve your seat in heaven, because it is not guaranteed at death. When we leave this life there is a forever awaiting us in one of two places; heaven or hell. The way we maneuver through this earthly life determines where we are reserving our seat in the forever life. *"And God raised us up with Christ and seated us with Him in the heavenly realms in Christ Jesus". Ephesians 2:6*

Note to self:

____

____

____

____

102

Cause vs. Effect

For it is God working in you, giving you the desire (will) and the power to do what pleases him. *Philippians 2:13*

The Holy Spirit gives us the ability to obey, or put into practice obedience. The Holy Spirit leading, works from the inside (heart), out. The Holy Spirt gives the ability to make the right decisions and the heart desires to be led, influenced, and coerced by the Holy Spirit. The outcomes, results, and consequences are then of good effect.

Note to self:

____

____

____

____

Where Love Lives

Love is another name for God. When we abandon, leave, turn a deaf ear and ignore his direction and commands; we are basically saying "love doesn't live here anymore". Making the choice to divide or divorce, separate, disconnect, disunite from the covenant of ourselves and God.

Renew your, "I do" to God and enter into a 'power pact' that is unbeatable, undefeatable, not divisible by enemies of God. Everything about God and what he does is motivated by love.

So we have come to know and to believe the love that God has for us. God is love, and whoever abides in love abides in God, and God abides in him. I John 4:16

Note to self:

____

____

____

____

Territory Taker

Possess the land, the promises of God, and destiny God has planned for you. *"Every place on which the sole of your foot treads I have given to you, just as I promised to Moses." Joshua 1:3*

God has not suggested but commanded us to claim and possess land he owns, take dominion over negative influences and claim spiritual territory for Christ. He has given us dominion over resources of which He is the source. *"The earth is the Lords the fullness thereof, they that live and dwell therein".Psalm 24:1*

We are blessed to be a blessing, not to justify aggression or self-serving motives and agendas.

Note to self:

____

____

____

____

108

Fear Steals Your Future

Fear is a basic human emotion we are allowed to feel but not dwell in. We are told to walk by faith, not feelings! We should go through fear to get to faith, on the other side – winning side = faith. Faith is a solid, like Christ the solid rock that will never fail us. Fear paralyzes not allowing movement or progress; while faith energizes, inspires and motivates to create. *"The Lord is my light and my salvation— whom shall I fear? The Lord is the stronghold of my life— of whom shall I be afraid?" Psalm 27:1*

Say hello to peace, joy, love, strength and hope – meaning welcome into my space.

Note to self:

____

____

____

____

Cruising Altitude

Cruising altitude is just what is says, the height at which an airplane flies or settles for most of the flight. It is good all around for the flight improving fuel efficiency, and avoiding adverse weather conditions, with little to no turbulence.

In order to go through life at cruising altitude, one must operate in the right attitude. Ever hear the saying that "your attitude determines your altitude", meaning the height you achieve in life is based on your attitude?

High altitudes can suffocate the average human, not inside an aircraft. If trying to reach heaven's heights or heavenly places, the realm where God dwells, one must believe in Jesus Christ and the power of salvation for which he gave his life.

"And what is the exceeding greatness of his power to us-ward who believe, according to the working of his mighty power." Which he wrought in Christ, when he raised him from the dead, and set him at his own right hand in the heavenly places." Ephesians 1:19-20

Note to self:

____

____

____

____

Sound Bytes

Sound travels or is transmitted in audible waves or vibrations. A sound bite is a striking, memorable statement, sentence or word worthy of quoting for TV news program; lasting under 8 seconds. Open your mouth and let a sound bite out, a scripture, and bite the enemy's ear. Sound has to travel through something or someone; might as well be you!

Ephesians 4:29: "Let no unwholesome word proceed from your mouth".

Note to self:

____

____

____

____

114

Artists

Rappers and lyricists are inspired writers, poets, creatives with skills and ability, and intellect to produce and think fast on their feet. Because we are all created by the creator – we all have creative ability. Know who you are and whose you are, and stop living beneath your privilege.

Of all God's creations, we humans, mortals; are the only ones created in His image and likeness. That is the greatest compliment he could have ever given us. Not only do we look like him; we were created with great care and attention, with power, authority and dominion to reign like him in this earthly realm. God calls us his masterpiece, a 'work of art', the 'apple of his eye'. He speaks well of us, and we should do the same and return the compliment.

"I praise you because I am fearfully and wonderfully made; your works are wonderful, I know that full well." Psalm 139:14

When in doubt as to who you are or will become; refer to the Word of God for a reminder.

Note to self:

____

____

____

____

More than Fond

Having an affection or being partially, enthusiastic about an individual will have your thoughts turn toward them periodically throughout the day. To love is a constant, intense, deep feeling – the very thought being a pleasure or delight.

Psalm 139:17 says, "How precious to me are your thoughts, O God! How vast is the sum of them!

The psalmist compares the amount of times God's thoughts turn towards us and trying to number would be like numbering granules of sand. It's enumerable, incalculable, manifold, untold; just how much he loves us!

Note to self:

____

____

____

____

Reckless Abandon

Total trust, leaving no room for doubt, nor regard for consequences for trusting. The majority serve an alternative god to Jesus Christ with reckless abandon or second thought for their sinful ways. It is second nature for humans to sin, be negligent, and live wild lives lacking caution. God desires us to love him with a reckless abandon, being transparent, open to receive love, and abandoning judgment and criticism of his Word.

"Whoever does not love does not know God, because God is love." I John 4:8

The all-encompassing, unconditional nature of God's love is 'reckless' in the sense of how freely he gives it to all, with no agenda or strings attached.

Note to self:

120

Temporarily on Hold

Sometimes a temporary hold can seem like forever. God's delay is not necessarily his denial. Learn to 'patiently wait' or pray for the discipline to 'patiently wait'. It produces strength, tenacity and the ability to soar like eagles over problems; looking at them through a different view or lens. It shifts the perspective and brings with it new insight as to how to move forward.

"But they that wait upon the Lord shall renew their strength; they shall mount up with wings as eagles; they shall run, and not be weary; and they shall walk and not faint." Isaiah 40:31

The temporary hold in God's timing and season for you is then accelerated or suspends actual time, so that you never miss a beat.

Note to self:

____

____

____

____

Ambient Sound

Balanced frequency over noise is called ambient sound or background sound that fills a space. Some are soothed, relaxed, and fall asleep by it. Examples being the sound of rain, wind, waves, seagulls, traffic or nature to name a few.

For me, it is God's still small voice. The whisper, subtle, quiet way God speaks to intentional, disciplined listeners in moments of stillness and reflection. When experiencing dramatic, traumatic events, purpose to listen for the still, small voice of God. What he is saying is by no means small, but constant movement, talking, and stirring can mute the sound.

"Be still, and know that I am God" Psalm 46:10
Note to self:

____

____

____

____

124

Intimate Contact

Intimate contact influences ones' soul. Be careful who you choose as a best friend, confidant, boyfriend, girlfriend, husband, wife, business partner, mentor, etc. Whether in an emotional, physical, or mental relationship, there is connectivity and sharing of thoughts, ideas, perspectives, intellect, etc.

Be sure God links you and not flesh, to ensure a lifelong healthy relationship; with Jesus Christ at the core.

"How can two walk together unless they agree" Amos 3:3

Note to self:

____

____

____

____

Acceptance Letter

Rejection is not a reflection of who you are; but a shadow of another's insecurity. Sometimes rejection is a way to be redirected on the path back to Christ. Get the lesson out of the non-acceptance or dismissal in whatever form it came. Whether you the individual were turned down, opinion dismissed, or your gift declined; know that you are welcomed with open arms and greatly loved by God.

Matthew 11:28: "Come to me, all you who are weary and burdened, and I will give you rest"

Come just as you are, no need to dress up or down or come toting a gift; you will be received, flaws and all.

Note to self:

____

____

____

____

128

Ask a Friend

Rash decisions are born out of anxiety and not well thought out. This is one of Satan's tactics to blindside us. When pressured, rushed, hurried; there is no time to consult God, get wisdom or counsel, or even to just think. Con artists, scammers, and fraudsters all operate like such, in order to take something of value from you. Recognize that God is present in your life at all times. Trust in the Lord with all thine heart; and lean not unto thine own understanding. *In all thy ways acknowledge him, and he shall direct thy paths. Proverbs 3:5-8*

Don't put any confidence or reliability in this flesh, especially when feeling anxious. Lean over and ask God his opinion like you would a friend.

Note to self:

____

____

____

____

130

Greatest Advocate Ever!

Jesus is seated at the right hand of God, because he finished his work at Calvary. Offering himself once and for all, as the sacrificial lamb. That's why he said at the cross, "it is finished", his work was complete. The priests in the temple never had chairs, due to their tasks being ongoing and constant – never finished.

We can stand in confidence that we now, have an advocate, someone fighting for us and pleading our case. That being Jesus Christ, supporting and backing us, saying *"forgive them Father for they know not what they do"! Luke 23:34 John 19:30*

Note to self:

____

____

____

____

132

Zip Lips

Our thoughts at times can be defiling due to their nature. The Word of God says they are important and can be controlled, made to come into alignment with the Word. When negative thoughts cross your mind, zip your lips, close your mouth, and do not speak them out. Once out, they cannot be taken back and can defile, soil, pollute, poison, or destroy the receiver as well as the giver. Just as oxygen makes cancer spread, so it is with negative words spoken out.

2 Corinthians 10:5: Take every thought captive to obey Christ

Note to self:

____

____

____

____

Blessings Cannot be Cursed

Blessings in the bible include but are not limited to God's favor, grace and protection, given to those who are obedient to his word. Sometimes blessings are given public notice of a favored status with God through prosperity and success. Satan curses while God blesses. However, when we choose to tolerate worldly practices and not speak out against evil – we conform. A blessing cannot be cursed, but can be corrupted through compromise.

Psalm 119:3: "Joyful are those who 'do not compromise with evil, and they walk only in his paths'"

Note to self:

____

____

____

____

Construction Zone

We are all a work in progress, meaning the transformation is ongoing. There are repairs being made, new structures being built, installation and modifications taking place. During this process, we are sometimes detoured, detained in a holding zone, or roads are totally blocked altogether. Whatever the case, yield where signs indicate, slow down, proceed with caution, and allow the construction to continue. The outcome is something new and better!

"Behold, I am doing a new thing" Isaiah 43:19

God is creating fresh beginnings, unexpected opportunities, and making ways of escape, as only he can do.

Note to self:

____

____

____

____

138

Submit Without Fear

Submission is to yield, which means to produce and provide. Submission is not for the faint of heart or weak. Only the strong and powerful can do a deep dive into the unknown, trusting enough to submit. Submarines go on sub-missions into deep under water for long periods of time. If it weren't for the vessels themselves encasing the crew, the immense water pressure would crush from the inside out, instantly killing. Submarines operate performing military missions without be noticed, attacking the enemy, gathering intelligence, deterring potential threats, doing research and protecting. These stealth missions are honored positions reserved for the powerful individual, empowered by submitting.

"Submit to God and be at peace with him; in this way prosperity will come to you". Job 22:21

Note to self:

____

____

____

____

Flashlight

Grace finds us no matter where we go, or what we do. Guilt and shame makes one go into hiding and never want to surface. Grace is a light sent from God, casting out all darkness; going into the tiniest of spaces and crevices. The grace light comes to reveal and heal, not condemn.

Ephesians 5:11–14 "Take no part in the unfruitful works of darkness, but instead expose them. Surrender to Jesus Christ and allow his redeeming love and light to shine through you."

Note to self:

142

Peace is Priceless

We can't afford to buy it nor live without it – peace that is. So how do we acquire it? Forgiveness is the key, forgiving others as well as yourself. You also have to not only look, search for it but pursue it, chase after it when it runs from chaos, confusion and unforgiveness. Some chase after gossip, discord, arguing and strife.

"Seek peace and pursue it" Psalm 34:14

The state of true happiness, bliss is found where peace dwells.

Note to self:

____

____

____

____

Vow of Falsehood

Pledging loyalty to a false god will incite fear and anxiety. Anxiety is a form of fear that overwhelms to the point of discomfort. Dedicating your loyalty to something powerless, mute, blind, deaf, inanimate, is blind faith in a created object! When in trouble, who will deliver you?

Psalms 135:15-18 The idols of the nations are silver and gold, made by human hands. They have mouths, but cannot speak, eyes, but cannot see. They have ears, but cannot hear, nor is there breath in their mouths. Those who make them will be like them, and so will all who trust in them.

Fear and Faith are polar opposites that cancel one another out.

Note to self:

____

____

____

____

146

Heads Up!

God is so protective and concerned about his children. He goes into battle on our behalf; walks in front of us acting as a shield. He picks us up and carries us when we get tired, acts as a coat when it's cold, places us up on a solid foundation when sinking or being bullied by the enemy. He keeps us a step ahead of the enemy; forewarned giving us a heads up.

Psalm 27:5 "For in the day of trouble he will keep me safe in his dwelling; he will hide me in the shelter of his sacred tent and set me high upon a rock.

He will place me out of reach on a high rock. Then I will hold my head high above my enemies who surround me.

He allows us to see the trap that awaits us and unravels the plots and schemes meant for our demise. Take heart, he never slumbers nor sleeps; always surrounds and protects.

Note to self:

____

____

____

____

148

Bones not Broken

We go through life sometimes sustaining injuries, getting bruised, cut, cursed out, spit on, ripped off, robbed; but we are still covered, Satan only allowed to go so far. This means the substantial part of us is kept intact, protected, and preserved. Jesus Christ, the sacrificial lamb, was tortured to death – but not one bone was broken! Jesus freely laid down his life so that he could redeem (regain possession, recover, reclaim) us and give us eternal life.

"He protects all his bones, not one of them will be broken."
Psalm 34:20
Note to self:

____

____

____

____

150

Home

Holy Spirit is part of the Godhead (Father, Son, Holy Spirit), that desires to dwell in a clean, well lit home. Darkness and sin is like living in the home of a hoarder, with mice secretly living beneath the mess. Make your heart a home that welcomes the Holy Spirit, clean and tidy, plenty Son-light shining brightly through, decorated with holy accessories. The sweet fruit of the spirit is available along with the sweet aroma of worship filling the space.

Then Christ will make his home in your hearts as you trust in him. Your roots will grow down into God's love and keep you strong. Ephesians 3:17-19

Note to self:

152

Grateful

Just a reminder to notice how easily the luxuries we've become accustomed to, can be taken away in an instant. The word of God instructs us to be thankful in all things, and as I grow in wisdom, I understand why. We don't recognize the luxuries we are afforded, until they are threatened or taken away. Something as simple as clean running water, something familiar and just plain expected for some; but for others, it is a miracle, a luxury. *"Rejoice always, pray continually, give thanks in all circum-*

stances; for this is God's will for you in Christ Jesus". I Thessalonians 5:18. Whatever it is you're doing, where ever you are, stop and just tell God 'thank you'.

Note to self:

____

____

____

____

154

Bloom where Planted

Fertile soil of the heart watered by the Word of God, full of nutrients needed to encourage growth. For as the soil makes the sprout come up and a garden causes seeds to grow, so the Sovereign LORD will make righteousness and praise spring up before all nations, Isaiah 61:11

Those that be planted in the house of the Lord shall flourish in the courts of our God. *They shall still bring forth fruit in old age; they shall be fat and flourishing, Psalm 92:13.* Communion with God, desiring to stay in his presence, are the right conditions and variables needed for a garden to flourish. We grow in grace and love when we allow ourselves to be rooted and grounded in His Word.

Note to self:

____

____

____

____

156

Actions Speak Loud

What we choose to believe shows up as fruit in our lives. We can say one thing but act in total contradiction. What will others believe – what we say or what we do? The answer is what we do – actions don't need a microphone; they are loud on their own. Actions are louder than the words you yell, scream, shout or roar.

Actions are fruit on a tree, coming from the seed planted in the heart.

Little children, let us not love in word or talk but in deed and in truth. I John 3:18

Note to self:

Heart Light

Our hearts house either darkness and heaviness or light and airiness; it's up to us. When God looks at us, he sees our hearts first, and where he is positioned in heaven, he can look to the earth and see either lit hearts or dark ones. Turn on your heart light today and allow love to lead like a flashlight. The opportunities to witness or introduce someone to Christ are endless. *"For the Lord sees not as man sees: man looks on the outward appearance, but the Lord looks on the heart".* Samuel 16:7. The only way we know what is in an individual's heart is by what they say and do. Show love today, and allow it to shine bright and light the way for someone to come to Christ.

Note to self:

____

____

____

____

Imitate Greatness

A wise man once said, "imitation is the sincerest form of flattery that mediocrity can pay to greatness" – Oscar Wilde

God is great and greatly to be praised; and we mere mortals are mediocre in comparison. If imitating someone is the best way to compliment them, then we should constantly imitate God. Show forth love and kindness to everyone, friend or foe, pray for the sick, feed the hungry, house the homeless, etc.

"The King will reply, 'I tell you the truth, whatever you did for one of the least of these brothers of mine, you did for me." Matthew 25:40

Let's compliment God today.

Note to self:

____

____

____

____

162

Look for God

Be attentive and intentional about looking for signs of God at work in your life. Is he bringing a new opportunity to transform, restore or renew you? Not all tests are trials; some are opportunities to bring about a change to introduce a new, transformed, better version of you. God wants to show you off, boast on you; in spite of you. You may not think yourself worthy, or that the strides you have made aren't large enough. Every step that gets you closer to God is a step toward reformation, transformation, and salvation.

"Behold, I am doing a new thing; now it springs forth, do you not perceive it?" Isaiah 43:19

Get out of your own way, and make way for God.

Note to self:

____

____

____

____

164

Daily Devotion

Daily devotion with God will bring dreams from your imagination into manifestation. Your devotion should include rehearsing God's Word, allowing it to become a part of you. It will then flow out of you like rivers of living water as a reflex reaction.

Just as we repeat our requests to God of the dreams we would like to see, repeat his word and watch it come to be! Your dreams that align with God's word will become a reality – from your imagination into manifestation!

"Whoever believes in me, as the Scripture has said, 'Out of his heart will flow rivers of living water." John 7:38

Note to self:

____

____

____

____

Master of Disguise

We should be careful with sizing someone up upon the first meeting. Some believe you only get one chance to make a great impression. The initial perception is crucial, but can often be skewed if based on shallow variables, such as designer shoes, clothing, car they drove up in, etc.

The enemy is a master at disguises and often dresses up mess to throw you off. His goal to steal, kill and destroy never changes and he didn't get the title 'master deceiver' or 'father of lies' without practice. He has perfected his craft! So try spirits by the Holy Spirit to see their place of origin. You belong to your father, the devil, and you want to carry out your father's desires. He was a murderer from the beginning, not holding to the truth, for there is no truth in him.

When he lies, he speaks his native language, for he is a liar and the father of lies. John 8:44 Beloved, believe not every spirit, but try the spirits whether they are of God: because many false prophets are gone out into the world. 1 John 4:1-5

The deception of wealth or epitome of health can be masks, worn to fool you.

Note to self:

____

____

____

Anger to Amazement

God will take the people who are angry at you and have them standing in amazement of you. Shedrach, Meshach, and Abed-nego trusted that God would deliver them out of any situation. So they disobeyed the king's commands about worshiping his god, and were thrown into a fiery furnace to die. When the king checked for their corpse, he saw God in the furnace with them, freely walking, unharmed by the flames; not even smelling of smoke!

The king, in his amazement, promoted them and decreed that anyone speaking against their God would be cut to pieces, and houses torn down. *Therefore, I decree that the people of any nation or language who say anything against the God of Shadrach, Meshach, and Abednego be cut into pieces, and their houses be turned into piles of rubble, for no other god can save in this way." Daniel 3:29*

This is how God makes your enemies react when you worship him in spirit and in truth.

Note to self:

____

____

____

____

Effortless Build

"*U*nless the LORD builds the house, they labor in vain who build it". *Psalm 127:1*

The amount of effort required to build anything is enormous; whether building a house, business, relationship, family, etc. The human venture, or endeavor necessary to build can exhaust the most experienced, educated and determined of individuals. No one wants to expend energy building, and it all be in vain, because we didn't consult God for his will or get his wisdom in the matter.

If you want true success in every part of life, consult God first – make him your project manager!

Note to self:

____

____

____

____

Peace Shoes

"*T*he law of his God is in his heart; his steps do not slip." Psalm 37:31 ". And how can anyone preach unless they are sent? As it is written, 'How beautiful are the feet of those who bring good news! Romans 10:15*

The soles of the feet control balance, posture and movement. When your feet are fit with the proper shoes, it makes the rest of the body come into alignment. Peace shoes have good grip to keep from slipping. Power, authority, submission and servitude are what is representative of the feet. When bringing good news of peace and salvation; run, don't walk in your 'peace shoes'.

Note to self:

____

____

____

____

Grace & Peace be Increased

Looking at your day in retrospect can sometimes bring thoughts of regret. Regret for something said, a decision or treatment rendered to someone. But God! He allows mercy to renew every morning, giving us a clean slate on which to start; and piles grace (unearned favor) upon the grace he already gave us. He loves us in spite of us! I'm thankful every day for knowing God doesn't hold it against us that we were born and shaped in iniquity; and sometimes prefers iniquity over purity.

Out of his fullness we have all received grace in place of grace already given. John 1:16

Note to self:

____

____

____

____

176

Insatiable Appetite

Appetites are never satisfied just like hell. Hell is said to be ever widening itself to make room for its occupants. Self-will and fleshly desires can lead astray to death of the soul, trying to satisfy it. Trying to fulfill impulses of the carnal nature also leads to death and destruction. Choose life and allow the influence of the Holy Spirit to lead, guide, and even convict when in error. A callused heart and spirit will numb to the point where sensation is deprived.

Ecclesiastes 6:7, "Everyone's toil is for their mouth, yet their appetite is never satisfied.

A heart massaged and guarded by peace will not harden.

Note to self:

____

____

____

____

178

Love is not a Battlefield

*M*ark 10:8 *"and the two shall become one flesh; so they are no longer two, but one flesh"*. The marriage covenant does not make one lose their identity. Marriage consummating takes care our innate need for love and to feel loved (intimacy). Don't allow your marriage to become a battlefield, harboring resentment, anger and bitterness; brought on through a spirit of competition. To be 'in love' is an experience that all should desire. Pursue 'real love', exampled by God the Father that unites reason and emotion, but requires discipline and effort (work). Love each other intentionally and with purpose.

Note to self:

Puzzle Pieces

We sometimes force the pieces of a puzzle to fit, but a beautiful picture or landscape it does not create. The piece can be a close match, but not the actual piece. Don't try to force God's hand, his plan, or will, to fit your life. Lay down your desires and embrace the purpose and place he wants for you. The more you surrender, the more beautiful the picture.

"For I know the plans I have for you," declares the Lord, "plans to prosper you and not to harm you, plans to give you hope and a future". Jeremiah 29:11

Note to self:

____

____

____

____

Loyalty is Royalty

Loyalty is strong feeling of support or allegiance which Mordecai and his cousin Queen Esther displayed. Mordecai remained loyal to his God and his people, even though a decree to destroy all of Jewish descent, had been signed and sealed. Mordecai, a man of regal character & nobility; while Queen Esther was a woman of God full of faith and grace.

Both Mordecai and Esther's loyalty paid off royally, as they were rewarded high positions of power and influence in the kingdom, for their saving efforts. *So the king took off his signet ring, which he had taken from Haman, and gave it to Mordecai; and Esther appointed Mordecai over the house of Haman. Esther 8:2 The Lord said to my Lord, "Sit at My right hand, Till I make Your enemies Your footstool." Psalm 110:1*

Pledge your allegiance to God only, and allow your enemies to be made a footstool!

Note to self:

____

____

____

____

What is your Leprosy?

We tend to judge and critique without knowing history, details, or facts. In the Old Testament, people did the same, just by an outward sign of leprosy on clothing or skin. Persons infected with leprosy showed skin lesions, boils, and rashes, which showed up on clothing as mold and on walls as mildew.

Leprosy symbolized, outwardly, that the individual or building was defiled due to some sort of sin. Leprosy is called Hansen's disease today and still is highly contagious and easily spread – just like sin! Just because sins aren't so public today doesn't lessen the severity of sin in general. Do a self-exam and make sure there are no secret sins lurking in your life.

Romans 3:23 "For all have sinned and fall short of the glory of God".

Sin is sin, whether done in private or made public by exposure.

Note to self:

____

____

____

____

About the Author

First Lady (Pastor) Kimberly Todd
Kimberly Todd assists her husband Karl Todd, Pastoring New Outlook Ministries and oversees the Women's Ministry, 'Princess of Providence'. She is the mother of two children, Karsten and Kayla; which she asserts as her profound signature achievement. She is a college graduate with a Bachelors' degree in Accounting and Psychology,

has over ten years work experience as a Social Worker, and is a licensed Real Estate Agent, as well as a licensed Christian Life Coach.

She has an incredible capacity for empathy, and compassion for others; prayerfully being their channel of blessing.

Her ultimate goal is to make relevant again the best book ever written – the Bible.